O LORD
NOT MORE VERSE!

by

John Gowans

Perhaps best known as the lyrics writer of the 11 Gowans/Larsson musicals, COMMISSIONER JOHN GOWANS here gives us the second collection of his poems to be published in the United Kingdom, a third having been produced in the USA. Like its predecessors, *O Lord, Not More Verse!* expresses spiritual truths with clarity and humour. As well as verse, this collection includes words of several songs written for particular occasions.

A Salvation Army officer since 1955, and accompanied since 1957 by his wife Gisèle, Commissioner Gowans has had wide experience in Britain, the USA Western Territory, France and the Australia Eastern/Papua New Guinea Territory – in the last two having served as territorial commander. Since April 1997 he has led the Army in the United Kingdom Territory with the Republic of Ireland.

O Lord, Not More Verse! is available as an audio-tape.

Cover Design by Jim Moss
Typeset and produced by THQ Print and Design Unit
Printed by Halstan & Co. Ltd., Amersham, Bucks., England

Contents

ii

O LORD

IT'S ME!

Unfinished Business

How many worlds
Did you make, Lord?
Not finished yet,
You say!
Still strewing stars
Like confetti
Out in your
Milky Way?

Marvellous, your creation.
Millions of stars I see;
Satellites of your glory,
Studding eternity!

Standing in awe and wonder,
Answer me if you can:
With all the worlds to think of,
Why do you think of man?

Tell me, O Lord Creator,
(Promise you will not smile!)
Why in your whole creation
Only mankind is vile?

I thought I heard you laughing?
How could I be so dim?
Where there's a man who'll let you,
You're still at work
On him!

Poor Relation!

You are my elder brother,
So Paul says!
That knocks me, let me tell you,
In a daze!
And I'm to be a son of God,
No less,
Though I may spell it
With a smaller 's'!
What have we got in common
You and I?
Can I be something like you
If I try?
The mere idea's enough
To set me chuckling.
You're beautiful, and I'm
An ugly duckling!

But we're related,
That at least I see,
For I can feel your Spirit
Move in me!

Inconsistency

He preaches like an angel,
Golden-voiced!
Before he's through
The driest eye is moist.
He woos and wins
The hardest heart
To you,
And in the pulpit
He's a giant, true!
But when he climbs down
From that vaulted place,
His attitudes wear
Quite a diff'rent face!
He's cold and distant,
Doesn't seem to care
How we are faring,
Hasn't time to spare.

His ways deny
The very truth he teaches.
Lord, help the man
To practise
What he preaches.

Why Me?

Find someone else!
Your files are full
Of super-gifted saints
Who'd love to do this job for you,
No groans and no complaints!
It's just not fair,
When you must have
A million men or more,
Your finger falls on me again,
Does no one keep the score?

Forgive me, Lord.
It's not by chance
You want me for this task.
Just call me any time you like,
You only have to ask.
With you there's no 'coincidence',
But only good design.
No doubt you have your reasons
Why the name you name
Is mine!

Music

Thank you for music –
Melodies that can't be
Overplayed.
Those harmonies that move my heart,
They cannot be man-made.

The way that music
Leaps through space
To come to stay with me,
Proves that it's more than human and
Divine it's got to be.

Such music finds the best in me
As nothing else can do
And brings me nearer
Truth itself,
And that means nearer you!

Trust

It's very sad,
But it was my mistake.
I trusted someone
And he let me fall.
I've got my bruises
But I'm wiser now.
I'll not trust him again,
Not him! That's all.

But this won't do,
For, Lord, how would it be
If you applied
The silly rule to me?

Replacement

You know I'm no Elijah,
I'm no prophet by profession,
But, Lord, I understand
His deep concern
For the succession.

I know I have a duty,
It's not simply
Self-effacement,
To talk about vocation
And to look for
My replacement.

But when I watch the miracle
Of young ones coming after,
I see I'm far too anxious,
My lament is turned to laughter.

How daft of me to worry,
My replacement I can see
Is wiser, nobler, and is made
Of better stuff than me!

Indiscriminate

There's a snob asleep
In the best of us,
And sometimes he shakes himself;
Insists that we take account of dress,
Of culture and wit and wealth;
And weigh the people we meet
With care
In the scales of creed and class;
And reckon as gold invaluable
The stuff that is only
Brass!

Please help us to follow you,
Lowly Lord,
You gladly went to dinner
With weird and wonderful
Way-out folk,
The taxman and
The sinner!

Invisible Support

I only *seem* to be alone.
I never am, I know.
You travel every road with me,
Go everywhere I go.
But when my faith is ambushed
And I have to stand and fight,
It's such a shame that you insist
On keeping out of sight.

You always fight beside me
When I come under attack.
Your 'straight right' puts
The strongest doubt
Or devil on his back –
They never know what hit them!
Is it part of your design
To give them the impression
That the knockout blow
Was mine?

Sower

The harvest is not mine to plan;
My job's to keep on sowing.
And what will prosper, this or that,
There really is no knowing.

Then let me sow with faith and hope,
And, if I must, with weeping,
Content because, just now and then,
You let me share the reaping!

Wilderness

This arid Arizona
Hurts my eyes ...
With all its burning sands
And brazen skies.
The rocks bake silently
Beneath the sun,
And never move –
Just as they've
Always done.

The stubby cactus,
Only barely green,
Attempts in vain
To civilise the scene.
Like some great animal
The landscape lies,
Clubbed into dumb submission
As it dies.

Yet, not entirely sterile
Is this land,
For mousy creatures stir
Beneath its sand.
The grey-green cactus too
Will have his hour,
And break, if briefly,
Into fiery flower.

No desert, so it seems,
Is quite deserted.
The grimmest knows
A little of your grace.
Help me detect your hand
At work upon it;
Discover beauty in
Its driest place!

Ever-Present

This dark cloud's been
Above my head
For ages now it seems.
The negatives
Of life came down
And crushed my dearest dreams.

The sad, the bad, the tragic
Darkly dominate my mind,
And no one cares a tinker's cuss,
Or bothers to be kind.

When I get out
From under this,
Lord, will I find you there
To calm my fears,
And dry my tears,
My celebration share?

I'm sure I'll find you waiting
And I'll feel your presence near,
For, now I think about it,
I can feel your presence here!

Self-Inflicted

Lead me not into temptation?
I'm not sure you ever do!
And it seems to me the trouble
Lies with me and not with you!

I surround myself with dangers,
Taking risks I need not take,
Then rely on you to save me
From the messes that I make!

Lead me not into temptation?
I am often so inane.
When I wander into danger,
Please, Lord, lead me out again.

Just Do It!

My heart has been stirred,
Your will has been heard,
I'll give you my word –
And just do it!

Committed today
To walk in your way
To hear what you say –
And just do it!

Whatever the task,
You've only to ask.
Whatever the cross –
Lead me to it!

Committed today
To walk in your way,
To hear what you say –
I'll just do it!

Calgary Stampede

His hat flew high
Into the air.
The bucking horse
Was mad.
The boy hung on
With all the skill
And all the strength
He had!
At last he landed
In the mud,
But heard above
The din,
He'd kept his seat
And held the reins
Just long enough
To win!

Give me the grace
When things are rough
To take it with
A grin,
And hang on
In adversity
Just long enough
To win!

Insulate

There's so much noise,
I'll have to find
A way to stop my ears.
The clamour for my mind,
My love, my time
And, yes, my tears,
Insists upon attention;
There are cries
I cannot drown.
For preservation's sake, Lord,
I must pull the shutters down!
I'll insulate my heart
From all that else
Will make it bleed;
Desensitise my mind
To all my brother's
Naked need.

Is it yourself
Who brings to me
A nagging kind of doubt
That in my haste
To save my skin,
I might have shut you out?

Impossible Demands?

To give you what I have
Is not a hardship.
My little all is yours,
Please take the lot!
The hardest thing to bear
Is that you ask me
For things which you know well
I haven't got!
But I have noticed, once
I am quite willing
To give you what I do not
Have in store,
You add to what I have
The wealth that's wanting.
I'm always rich enough
To give you more.

I Know Where You Live

(Revelation 2:13, *NEB*)

Do you know where I live?
Where I have to dwell?
Often it's like Heaven,
Sometimes it's like Hell!
Evil lives where I live,
Fighting to get in;
And I battle daily
With all sorts of sin.

Do you know where I live?
Do you know the folk
I'm supposed to lead, Lord?
Really, it's no joke!
Petty people often,
Quarrelsome and blind;
Sometimes so appealing,
Sometimes so unkind!

Do you know where I live?
What I have to face?
Questions with no answers!
Problems pack the place!
Sometimes things go smoothly,
Sometimes like a dream.
Mostly it's just bedlam
And I want to scream!

Child, I know where you live,
I live there as well,
And I go where you go;
I'm Immanuel!

Give Way!

Help me to do all I can do,
Give what I've got.
You'll make good use of it, I know;
It's not a lot!
But when I'm old and past it,
Help me please
To bring the hurt to you
Upon my knees.
Then get up with a smile
Upon my face,
And give the younger man
My precious place!

Not only help me grin,
Lord, when he scores,
But make me want
To start up
The applause!

For Them

I put my hands together
And I stand
Before your throne.
Just me!
And yet there's more than me;
In fact I'm not alone!
Behind me stands
A motley crowd.
I want to speak for those
Who give themselves
In service
For the nameless no one knows.
Your servants
Who spend all they have,
And sometimes something more,
In drying tears,
And calming fears,
And often waging war
On poverty, on loneliness,
On hopelessness and grief,
On sadness and on badness,
Never asking for relief.

Please give your willing ones
The strength
And all the grace they need.
I can't do much to help them,
I can only
Intercede.

O hear me, Lord.
Be near them, Lord.
For *them* I pray this prayer.
And, when they need you
Most of all,
Just let them know
You're there!

Rough Diamond

I want my way,
I confess it!
I'm even fool enough
To think my way is best,
Until I take a sickle
To my harvest
And return with
Empty, blighted ears –
And full eyes!

Yet there lies
Embedded in my obstinacy
That bright stone
Determination,
Semi-precious thing,
Which, cut by Christly hands,
May sparkle yet
When set
Into the silver of
Your will for me!

You Win!

This battle's gone on long enough,
And I can fight no more.
We've had so many skirmishes
I haven't kept the score!

Oh, I've succeeded now and then
To dash the plan you planned.
But soon or late, I've felt the weight
Of your restraining hand!

I've silenced you a time or two;
It wasn't any good,
For you found other ways to make
Your signals understood.

Now I surrender. Occupy
What anyway's your own.
And make my heart your habitat,
Or better still – your throne!

Afraid to Ask

I do not pray,
Because I know you'll answer!
I dare not ask,
For then I would receive!
My silence is not proof
That I am faith-less —
It only goes to show that I believe!

I do not seek
For fear that I might find you;
And finding YOU
Might well mean losing ME!
And if I knocked, of course
The door would open!
And I would have to enter, don't you see?

Give me the nerve
To knock, to seek, to ask, Lord;
To enter in,
To find and to receive,
I don't doubt for a moment
You will answer.
I tremble, Lord, because I *do* believe!

Unless You Come . . .

'Go ye therefore ... and, lo, I am with you'
(Matthew 28:19-29, *AV*)

Unless you come with me
I will not go.
My promises are nothing without yours.
I know I've vowed away
My life, my strength, my very will,
But I will break it all unless
You come with me.

Unless you come
I'll lean upon myself
And then I'll fall,
And men will laugh
At you as well as me, which would be
More than I could bear.
I shall be full of confidence –
Empty of power;
I shall seem strong –
But melt in the first heat.

If you will come,
And I am sure you will
For you promised,
Then I will go.
It will be easy for me.
No, not easy –
Possible.

Tears

The sad, sad sobs that say
Some heart is hurt
Spur me to action, a
Strange strength exert.
The bitter breaths of pain
Distilled as tears,
The molten misery,
The liquid fears
Have power to push me where
I would not go;
Discover depths in me
I did not know!

Tell me, O Christ, am I
Most truly yours
When pity batters down
My battened doors;
When I forget to pose
And, frantic, feel
The pain of someone else,
Its pointed steel:
And know my brother's or
My sister's cares:
And simply, only, mix
My tears with theirs?

Best Gift

I gave my friend my wisdom,
I advised him.
I gave him my attention,
My concern.
I gave him of my time
And of my talents.
I taught him ev'rything
That he could learn!
I gave him hospitality,
I fed him.
I gave him all I had,
My total wealth,
But still deprived him
Of the thing most needed.
I gave him all I had,
But kept myself!

Now, though I have no strength
That I can give him,
No cleverness,
No wisdom, and no wealth,
My friend with gratitude
Receives me gladly –
For I give nothing now
Except myself!

Bridge

I want to be a bridge
Though I'm not strong.
I want to be a bridge
So wide, so long
That over me from doubt
To faith may pass
The lad in search of God,
The seeking lass.

Put steel into my faith,
And concrete too,
That men may travel
Over me
To you!

Any Time

It's the work of a moment,
It's the work of a lifetime!
It is born in an instant,
It may take eternity.
But the work of the Spirit,
Of the transforming Spirit,
Can begin at this moment
In me!

Continuation

Is this the end?
Should I be scared
Of my friend Death?
No! I'm prepared.

I'm quite at peace,
From fear set free,
Convinced of
Continuity

In Christ! . . . In Christ! . . . In Christ! . . .

O LORD

IT'S CHRISTMAS!

Christmas Box

How can I thank you for this Gift sublime,
This wrapped divinity,
Parcelled infinity?
What can I give of value that is mine,
To show my gratitude,
Define my attitude?

I have no wisdom, and I have no wealth.
I'll give myself!

It's Time

I don't want to disturb you,
Holy Child upon the hay,
So peacefully asleep,
But I'm afraid it's Christmas Day.
I don't want to disturb you
But I dare not let you sleep;
Your diary's full already
Of appointments you must keep.
Already in your tiny hands
The nail-prints I can see.
I don't want to disturb you
But it seems it has to be.

I wish there was some other way.
I often wonder why
To dry the tears of all the world
A Baby has to cry?

Incarnation

The baby cries again this year,
As ev'ry year!
And I must think of God in Christ.
Again I fear
And comprehend, that's if I can,
How God could wrap himself in man!

If God should want to speak to man,
Say something good,
The words he chose would have to be
Well understood.
One single lovely Word he said
And laid it in a manger bed.

If I have grasped the truth at all,
I've understood
That God once dressed himself in man,
In flesh and blood,
And crossed the gulf of time and space
And came to join the human race!

My finite mind and fumbling thoughts
Still find it hard
To grasp the message printed on
My Christmas card:
That God's sublime salvation plan
In Beth'lem's borrowed barn began!

I can't explain the ageless truth
Of love expressed;
I only know – in Jesus all
The world is blessed.
And when I look into his face
I'm glad God joined the human race!

Mercy Seat?

Is this the mercy seat,
This manger place
Which seems so full of love,
Of good, of grace?

And will God talk to me,
Tell me his will,
Here, wrapped in silences,
So soft, so still?

I touch this tiny hand,
I see this face;
The God I'm looking for
Is in this place.

My heart prepares itself
Its Lord to greet,
And kneels with joy before
This mercy seat.

And must I bring a gift,
Some worth, some wealth?
Is it enough for me
To give myself?

Give him your yesterdays,
Tomorrows too.
He asks for nothing else
But you!
Just you!

Surprised

I don't know quite what I should say
As I kneel down upon the hay
Which clothes the floor but cuts my knees.
Would someone like to help me please?

I came to say hello to God,
And took the trail the wise men trod.
They seemed to think they knew the way,
And I'd prepared some things to say.

But now I'm taken by surprise,
In fact I can't believe my eyes.
To think that men make such a fuss
For Someone who looks so like us!

Two hands, two feet, two eyes, one nose ...
But something special I suppose
Has somehow slipped inside the wrappings;
How else explain the angel-trappings?

Is God himself inside this Child?
Can God almighty be so mild?
I do believe the Baby smiled!

Rule Britannia

The Britisher at Bethlehem still wears his bowler hat,
And asks politely for some tea, with muffins and all that!
You would not call him pious, but he knows how things should be;
He lays his rolled umbrella down and drops upon his knee
With wiser men upon the hay.
'God save the Queen' – you'll hear him pray!

The Britisher at Bethlehem his carols loves to sing,
And with the Sally Army band he greets the infant King.
He eats too much, he spends too much, he gives too much away,
With all the glee of childhood counts the hours till Christmas Day;
And be he Irish, Welsh or Scot,
He thanks the Lord for what he's got!

The Britisher at Bethlehem can hear the abbey bell
Reminding him it's Christmas, whilst Big Ben will hourly tell
That politics and parliaments have but the briefest day,
And Downing Street will call upon its countrymen to pray!
Then Labour, Tory, Democrat
Will bow his head and doff his hat!

The Britisher at Bethlehem, if taken by surprise,
Is found to be quite moved, though he'll say, 'Smoke gets in your eyes,'
And fumble for his handkerchief and loudly blow his nose.
It's not polite to tell him that his deep emotion shows!
'I'm not religious, friend,' he'll say.
But it's a lie on Christmas Day!

Ode to the Christmas Kettle

I can't say that you're elegant,
You're often kind of battered,
More practical than pretty I would say!
But people sing your praises,
You must feel kind of flattered.
You're really rather famous in your way.

It's true that when you first appeared
Some sniggered and some even sneered;
To find you squatting on the sidewalk
Provoked a certain silly snide-talk!

I've noticed that you travel now,
And everywhere we find you:
Hong Kong and Santiago, Paris, Rome;
Yours is the place of honour,
Nobody seems to mind you,
And anywhere you seem to be at home.

First Ladies, and bag-ladies too,
All seem to make a fuss of you.
We're glad your stock is flying high,
The only limit is the sky!

What really matters, you'll agree,
Is not your reputation,
But that your work for Others* is
Endorsed by ev'ry nation.
Once more this year we'll ring your bells,
Fill you with money from 'the swells',
To give the folk in need a break,
And do it all for Jesus' sake!

* 'Others' was the single word contained in a New Year's
greeting said to have been sent by William Booth to
Salvationists around the world

41

O LORD
IT'S YOUR WORLD!

Homeless

He has no home except this grimy street
Which wears the winter like a shapeless shroud.
He has no friend, except the witless one
Who walks beside him through the thoughtless crowd.

He has no food but what his fingers find
Among the garbage which the dogs disdain.
He has no hope to help him through the day,
No one to ease the lonely night of pain.

Does no one care? Is no one moved enough
To throw a blanket round his bony form?
Will no one put some bread into his hand,
Protect his head against the stinging storm?

I care! . . . says Christ. I know what 'homeless' means.
I'm with the hungry in the line for beans!
I know the pitted pavement of the street,
And Skid Row bears the imprint of my feet.
I've often had no place to lay my head;
At Bethlehem they borrowed me a bed!

You want to find me? Then you'd better come
And face the stinking of the city slum,
Where men live daily wishing they were dead,
And give away their dignity for bread.

You have the gall to ask me if I care?
Come down to Desp'rate Street, you'll find me there!
And grasp this truth, for it could set you free:
All that you do for them, you do for me.

In the Bar

She took the gospel paper
In her ringed and bangled hand
And ripped it down the middle
With a smile!
Her painted eyes flashed out
In purpled splendour touched with green –
And held my startled gaze
For just a while.

I murmured, 'Well, God bless you!'
And words would come no more.
But what was I to say to such
A brazen kind of whore?

My memory of the moment
Gives me still a twinge of pain.
Please tell me what to say,
Lord, when I meet that girl again!

The End?

I closed his eyes.
'He's gone,' I said,
And really I was glad.
But turning to his daughter,
Who was deaf and strained
And sad,
I had to shout the news again,
'He's left us, dear. He's dead.'
She read my lips and understood,
And then she dropped her head.
I felt ashamed,
For though I'd vigiled
With her through the night,
I'd done it as a duty
But I'd hardly shared her plight.
My platitudes were useless
Till I gently touched her cheek,
And then her sadness reached me
And I didn't have to speak.

Lord, help me minister to men
With heart as well as hand.
And share the pain of others
In a way they understand.

When God Expressed Himself

When God expressed himself
The Word he spoke
Was clearly understood
By ordinary folk.
They looked into his eyes,
One single look sufficed;
Men read the mind of God
In the face of Christ.

When Christ laid down his head
Upon a manger bed,
His coming simply said:
God is with man!
Kneeling upon the hay,
We hear the Baby say:
Your God is here to stay;
God is with man!

When Christ was crucified
And hung his head and died,
His silenced body cried:
God loves like this!
And still to us today
Two thousand years away,
His suff'rings simply say:
God loves like this!

Better World

This broken world in shattered fragments lies.
From ev'ry corner hear its children's cries;
Its famished millions ask in vain for bread;
The very souls of men are left unfed.
The Saviour calls for saviours, in his name
To take the broken bits and build again.

Among the ruins of what might have been,
And in the darkness where no hope is seen,
Illuminate the cross where Jesus died.
Disclose his love which cannot be denied.
Go spend yourselves in service for the lost,
And like your Lord, refuse to count the cost!

Faith

There is a time for tears,
A time for sighing;
There is a place for grief,
A place for crying.
But in the mystery of
Unanswered prayers
Let faith hold fast to this:
God cares!

The sun won't always shine,
Sometimes the rain clouds form
And from the once-clear sky
May fall the thunderstorm.
The unexpected stress
Awakens sleeping fears,
And faith must find its way
Through mists of bitter tears.

It's easy to believe
In providential care
When faith is still untried
By doubt and black despair.
But in the longest night,
When fear and pain are real,
There faith will prove itself,
Its hidden strength reveal.

There is a time for tears,
A time for sighing;
There is a place for grief,
A place for crying.
But in the mystery of
Unanswered prayers
Let faith hold fast to this:
God cares!

The Healer

In the quiet of evening
At the close of the day,
When men's thoughts soar in silence
And it's easy to pray,
Then they brought to the Healer
Those who needed his care,
And they all had an answer
To their prayer!

So they brought him the leper
With his sores open wide,
And they carried the weakest
And the worst to his side;
And they brought the blind beggar,
The lame man with his crutch;
And they all claimed the healing
Of his touch.

With their burns and their bruises,
With their wants and their woes,
They were brought to the Healer
Who the remedy knows;
And they came with their sorrows,
They were sick, they were sad,
But the touch of the Healer
Made them glad.

In the quiet of evening
At the close of the day,
As our thoughts soar in silence
And it's easy to pray,
We can bring to the Healer
Those in need of his care,
And we'll all have an answer
To our prayer!

51

For Their Sakes

(John 17:19, *AV*)

Aware of all the sorrows that surround me,
Of all the pain, the suff'ring, the distress;
Conscious of evil in the world around me,
And powers diabolical, no less,
I see the sea of faces marked by sadness,
The tide of wickedness, ill-will, ill-health;
Though conscious of my limited resources,
For their sakes I would sanctify myself.

I see the fam'ly, bruised and sometimes broken;
I see the elderly, afraid, alone;
I see the adolescent in his anguish
Looking for easy answers, finding none;
I see the single-parent with the children,
Close to the brink of dangerous despair;
Where there is want and wickedness and weakness,
I want to go for you. Lord, send me there!

I don't suppose that I can make a diff'rence,
The miracle they need is never mine.
But if you send me, that means you'll come with me,
The human will be linked with the divine.
My hands are holy even though they're human,
When with them other hungry ones are fed.
The food I offer in your name is sacred
And it becomes your wine, your broken bread.

Peace?

Your will is peace?
We wonder then
Why is your world
War-torn,
When long ago
In Bethlehem
The Prince of Peace
Was born?

Is it because
There's still no room
Within the hearts of men
For one who wants
To calm our storms
And bring us peace
Again?

Peacemakers, Lord,
We want to be:
Help us in all we do
To make men see
That there's no hope
Of peace
Outside of
You!

The Stones Cry Out

My Lord, you speak in ev'ry flow'ring tree,
In ev'ry leaf your voice is heard;
I walk alone beside the restless sea
And ev'ry wave becomes your word;
The humming bee
Sings just for me
Of your sublime divinity.

The lightning's flash, the thunder's crash
Pronounce your majesty.
The very grass won't let me pass
But speaks of you to me.
Shall I alone be silent then?
Not sing my song of praise?
No! Let my being be for you
And sing you all my days.

My Lord, you live in ev'ry lovely thing,
And ev'ry shape your beauty shows.
Because of you the world is wonder-full,
The grass is green, the rose is rose;
Each beating wing,
Each creeping thing,
Cannot be silenced, has to sing!

The lightning's flash, the thunder's crash,
Pronounce your majesty.
The very grass won't let me pass
But speaks of you to me.
Shall I alone be silent then?
Not sing my song of praise?
No! Let my being be for you
And sing you all my days.

In this quiet moment, still, before your throne,
Conscious of your presence, knowing I am known,
In this quiet moment set my singing free;
In this quiet moment, make a better me!

Lord, let my being speak of you,
My living be your praise;
And let my spirit sing for you,
Proclaim your wonder-ways,
That men may all your glory see,
Breathe all your beauty into me;
Let me adore you with my days
And ev'ry part of me be praise.

Hope

Hope, like a candle, lightens the darkness,
Flickering, fragile flame;
Hope, like a lantern, cancels the darkness,
Always remains the same.

Hope, like the sunrise, scatters the shadows,
Darkness resists in vain;
Nothing can crush it, nothing can kill it,
Buried – it lives again!

Christ is the candle; Christ is the lantern;
Christ the eternal flame;
Christ is the sunrise, scatt'ring our shadows;
Christ is the hope of men!

Buried – he lives again!

O LORD

WE'RE YOUR PEOPLE!

An Earthen Jar

You're not to boast about your gifts,
Though you have many –
And don't suppose you're made of better stuff
Than those who haven't any.

An earthen jar – that's you!
But holding treasure
Which God entrusts to you
In generous measure.

The wonder is
That he should choose you out
To hold his gifts –
With better jars about!

Sons of God

Now are we the sons of God!
Unfinished, uncompleted;
But he who reigns within our hearts
Shall never be defeated,
Till by his Spirit he refines
The work he has begun,
And in our human faces shines
The beauty of his Son.

Now are we the sons of God!
Resembling in our fashion
The first-begotten Son of God
In purity and passion.
His holiness, his humbleness,
Sincerity serene,
Shall by his Spirit's presence
In our lesser lives be seen!

Now are we the sons of God!
In spite of human failing;
The pow'r of God at work in man
Is everywhere prevailing.
Imperfect samples of his grace
We still proclaim his story;
Incarnate in the sons of men
Are glimpses of his glory.

Now are we the sons of God!
The fam'ly likeness bearing,
The foll'wers of the Son of God
His saviourhood are sharing.
Blind to their selfish wantings
And disdainful of disaster,
In selfless service they become
A little like their Master.

Sincerely Yours

Amazed that from the mass of men you call me,
O Christ divine,
Of timeless truth to be your true proclaimer,
This call is mine;
Sent by yourself, devoted to your cause,
In word, in deed, in truth,
Sincerely yours!

Convinced that you have chosen me to serve you,
And you alone,
All other claims upon my time, my talents,
I now disown;
Deaf to the world's disdain or its applause,
In word, in deed, in truth,
Sincerely yours!

I dedicate my all to you,
What you dictate I'll gladly do,
And where you send with joy I'll go,
Your promised presence daily know.
Devoted to your cause,
Sincerely yours!

Self-Denial

She: Do yer think it matters, dear (she said),
      That little children cry for bread
      In distant places?
      And do we really have to care
      That men are killing men somewhere
      With coloured faces?

He: We ought,
      Old sport!

She: It all seems such a frightful bore
      That foreign folk will go to war,
      And mis'ries mount;
      And little lads don't know their letters
      And think that those are twice their betters
      Who can count. (She sighs)

He: You might not give a tinker's cuss,
      And ask what it's to do with us.
      We're here! They're there!
      But worshipping with words won't do
      A thing for God or me or you,
      Unless we care.

      The only way to do God good
      Is just to act the way we should
      Toward each other.
      And every man, I mean to say,
      Though maybe half a world away,
      Is still my brother.

She: It's such a bother tho', my dear,
      When I would rather think of here
      And you and me,

That I must think of them and there,
And give much more than I can spare
To charity!

But I'm not dim and I have seen
That truest worship may well mean
The death of 'me'.
Not just what's said upon the knees,
But what's done for 'the least of these'
Will set us free.

He: That's right,
      Delight!

It's All Right to Cry

It's all right to cry – but not to despair,
For if we reach out we'll find Jesus there;
The darkness may shadow the brightest of days,
But Jesus is near to the person who prays.

It's human to sigh. It's human to weep,
When wounds are still new and desp'rately deep.
But God hasn't altered whatever man says,
And Jesus is near to the person who prays.

He cares when we cry. He shares our distress,
And even our tears he's willing to bless;
He comes when we call him, he never delays,
And Jesus is near to the person who prays.

It's all right to cry. Reach out in the night,
Your Saviour is near, though hidden from sight;
The songs of your sorrow he'll turn into praise,
For Jesus is near to the person who prays.

Demonstrate!

It's not enough to say it,
You must sing it!
You must shout it!
If you've really got religion
You must tell the world about it!
If God has gotten to you,
And your heart's as white as snow,
Don't keep the secret to yourself,
Let everybody know!

> You've got to demonstrate,
> You've got to shout aloud,
> You've got to get the message to the crowd;
> Let's have a thousand trumpets and a thousand drums,
> And let's be fools for Jesus until Jesus comes.

> Take the biggest hoarding,
> Hire the biggest hall,
> Wave the biggest banner,
> Sound the trumpet call!
> Use the brightest music,
> Call the bravest men,
> Make the worst take notice
> That God cares for them!

It's not enough to say it,
You must write it,
You must roar it!
For what's the use of goodness
If you bottle it and store it?
Let's get out on the street,
Invade the tavern and the dive,
Tell men there's a Saviour,
And that Saviour is ALIVE!

A New Race Shall Arise

In the pow'r of the Spirit a new race shall arise
With the beauty of Jesus all ablaze in their eyes;
And a garden shall flourish where the desert has been,
And the plan of creation be no longer a dream.

In the pow'r of the Spirit a new race shall arise;
They'll be generous and gentle, they'll be winsome and wise;
They'll be something like Jesus in compassion and grace,
And the cost of their calling they'll be glad to embrace.

In the pow'r of the Spirit a new race shall arise;
They'll make friends of the people other people despise.
And with truth they shall triumph over all that is wrong,
And the plan of redemption is the theme of their song.

> And transfigured men shall transform the earth,
> Build a better world, bring a second birth;
> People prize again what is pure and true,
> And the world of men shall be made anew!

With the beauty of Jesus all ablaze in their eyes,
In the pow'r of the Spirit a new race shall arise!

If I Be lifted Up . . .

(John 12:32, *AV*)

It is not, Lord, that we would bring you down,
Take hold of holy things with hasty hand
And bear them low, and lower, till they reach
That sunken place, where unrepentant stand
The sons of men.

It is not, Lord, that we would force men's faith,
And in unconsecrated bread and wine
Bring you to them, and press unwilling lips
To taste, at least, communion divine.

It is not, Lord, that we would lure men to
Their highest good, or coax them to the cross,
Or bribe them with the promise of great gain,
Flaunting the profit, covering the loss.

But we would lift you up, that seeing you
Men shall be drawn to leave their self-made slum,
And toss their tawdry treasures to the dust,
And claim their right, through your power, to become
The sons of God.

Kingdom

He is not King
Till we give him his Kingdom;
He has no throne
Until we give up ours!
Unless we make him room,
The Christ is homeless.
Unless we let him reign,
He has few powers.
He is not truly King
Until we crown him
The Lord of all we have,
Our hopes, our schemes.
And then our ugliness
Is touched with beauty
And loveliness beyond
Our wildest dreams!

Yours!

If I have any voice, it's yours, Lord; use it
To tell of your compassion and your care;
To talk of new beginnings, resurrections,
Announce your patient kindness everywhere.

If I have any strength, it's yours, Lord; use it
To work for others, careless of the strain;
To carry heavy burdens for my brothers,
And when they fall to lift them up again.

If I have any tears, they're yours, Lord; use them
To take away the hurts that others feel;
To demonstrate the depths of your compassion,
And touch the hearts that only you can heal.

If I have any gifts, they're yours, Lord; use them
For God's sole glory . . . not for my applause;
The talents I may have I never earned, Lord;
You gave them to me once, and they're still yours!

Free Will

Faced with the choice, I choose your way, not mine!
All voices silence but the voice divine;
The plans I've planned surrender at your call,
With your designs I will replace them all,
Renounce my will, my lawful rights refuse.
Faced with the choice, with joy, your way I choose!

Who would proclaim a liberating gospel,
Must first himself its fright'ning freedom feel.
He who declares the pow'r of God to change men,
Know for himself that transformation real.
Faced with the choice, he yields himself to you,
Your will, O God, throughout his life to do.

Though far from faultless, take the gift I offer,
This living gift of 'me' accept to use.
Faced with the choice, I turn from *my* ambitions,
Your will for me with tranquil heart to choose;
Called to your service, this alone I ask:
Lord, make your servant equal to the task!

Pledged to proclaim this liberating gospel,
Called to announce the news men long to hear,
Before the awesome task, O God, I tremble;
My faith is frail, although my call is clear.
But where you send I'll go and faithful be,
Since where you send I know you'll go with me!

Not Our Prisoner

God's not the pris'ner of our precious laws,
Confined to work in ways
We understand.
Upon the face of earth his finger draws
Surprising patterns which his
Heart has planned.

God's not the captive of confining creeds;
He breaks the bound'ries of
The narrow mind.
Our finite fancies he by far exceeds,
And yet, like any father,
He is kind.

God's not restricted by our rigid rules;
He smiles at our attempts
To chain him fast.
Our favourite frames of ref'rence ridicules.
The last is first with him,
The first is last!

Suddenly

'The Lord, whom ye seek, shall suddenly come to his temple'
(Malachi 3:1, *AV*)

Suddenly come to your temple, I pray,
Meet with your people who seek you today;
This is your house, sanctify it anew,
It is your own, Lord, we give it to you.

Not made with hands are your temples, I know,
Guest of the heart where compassion can grow,
Coming with peace now your power impart,
Take up your residence here in my heart.

Now as the gift of your presence I sense,
Break through my pride and its silly pretence,
Suddenly come, I your temple would be,
Bring in your beauty and live within me.

Free?

Your service, Lord, they say is perfect freedom.
It's true that I'm allowed a lot of choice!
In many things it seems you've no opinion –
At any rate I do not hear your voice.

I please myself a thousand times unbridled.
Large areas are simply left to me!
Quite unadvised, you trust me to choose wisely,
But Master, please, I don't want to be 'free'!

When most I need you, let me hear your whisper
Which pours your wisdom in my willing ear,
Directing me in making 'my' decision,
For that's the way I like it, have no fear!

It's true, of course, that there is no coercion.
You never force my hand or threaten me;
The fact I choose obedience alters nothing,
Who calls you Master is for ever free!

Dictation

Dictate the message that
Is needed now!
Make clear your meaning and
Then tell us how
Through print and paper we
May make it plain;
Bring muddled man back to
The truth again.

With pencil poised your people
Wait your word,
That in your world
Your message may be heard,
Your word of truth for now,
Your word of light;
Help us to hear it first
And then to write!

Wedding

With joy, O Lord, here in your house
We make our prayer,
Please will you walk through life with us
Our journey share,
And then, whate'er the future brings,
You will be there!

With thanks, O Lord, we now look back
To yesterday,
And trace the times you guided us
Along the way,
And kept us when alone we might
Have gone astray.

With peace, O Lord, we here commit
Our lives to you;
Our health, our hopes, our happiness,
Ambitions too;
To all the vows we make today
Please keep us true.

A Wedding Prayer

We're ordinary people,
And we have no right or claim
To any kind of favours,
But quite simply,
In your name,
May we suggest that daily,
Through the good times
And the bad,
When life is full of laughter
But especially
When we're sad,
You make your presence
Real to us
In some quite special way,
And then we know
For certain
That we won't go
Far astray!

And at that special moment
We shall close our eyes
And pray,
And place our hands
In yours again,
Just as we do
Today!

Co-Workers

God is building his Church,
And because of his grace
In the work of construction
We all have a place.
We can bring him our talents,
Our gifts and our skills,
Help to build up his Church
In the way that he wills.

God is building his Church,
His temple, his throne,
And we're his co-workers,
His people, his own!

People of Power

Called into being by his Holy Spirit,
Shaped by his Spirit, by his Spirit fed,
God made an army, Army of Salvation,
Bound to his bidding, by his Spirit led.
His was the glory! His was the power!
His people, they became the people for the hour.

Moved with compassion, sincere in their service,
Pledged and committed, counting not the cost,
God's selfless soldiers, spent all, asking nothing,
Healing the wounded, seeking for the lost.
Touched by his Spirit, armed with his power,
His people proved to be the people for the hour.

Still children suffer, helpless in their hurting,
Still faith is needed, kindliness and care;
Still there is sadness, evil goes unchallenged,
Deep is the darkness round us everywhere.
Hear our petition! Pour out your power!
And make your people, Lord, the people for this hour.

Lord of our yesterdays, be with us yet;
All of our modern needs in you are met;
Filled with your Spirit, charged with his power,
O make your people, Lord, the people for this hour!